# GOOD VIBES WITH DR. S

*Light, Love, and Life*

DR. RANDOLPH D. SCONIERS (DR. S)

# Dedication

This book is dedicated to my wife Yini and my three daughters Jazlyn, Destiny, and Alina. You guys are always my inspiration and provide me with the positive energy to write freely and from a place of peace and compassion. I would also like to give my daughter, Destiny a special acknowledgement for taking the photographs of me for the back cover of this book. I know she's smiling ear to ear seeing this credit! I love you guys forever!

-Dr. S but to you guys, Papi

# Contents

INTRO .......... 1

DO NOT ROB YOURSELF OF PEACE, BY LIVING WITH REGRETS. .......... 3

PRIORITIZING ME! A COMMITMENT TO MY SELF-CARE. .......... 13

I AM COOL WITH CHANGE. IT IS THE CHANGING PART THAT'S TOUGH FOR ME. .......... 20

FORGET OUTSIDE, THERE'S INSIDE WORK TO DO! .......... 27

DO NOT WALK AWAY FROM YOUR PURPOSE! .......... 33

KEEP YOUR APOLOGIES...CHANGE YOUR BEHAVIOR! .......... 39

WE ALL NEED SOME R & R! "RELATIONSHIP RECIPROCITY". .......... 45

COGNITIVE CRISIS: "KEEP YOUR MIND RIGHT"! .......... 53

TRIGGERED AGAIN...BUT I AM STILL HEALING! .......... 62

"THANK YOU FOR THE OPPORTUNITY BUT I QUIT"! A 4-WEEK LESSON ABOUT PURPOSE. .......... 68

THE DREAMER'S DILEMMA? .......... 74

STOP WAITING FOR APPROVAL! .......... 79

HIP-HOP AND MENTAL HEALTH: THE BRIDGE NOBODY WANTS TO BUILD....SO IT SEEMS?! .......... 87

IF YOU ARE BEING STRETCHED, PULLED, AND PRESSED...JUST STAY RIGHT THERE! (GROWING PAINS). .......... 93

THE PERFECT LOVE STORY.... STARRING YOU! .......... 98

DO NOT HATE THE STORMS, WHILE WAITING ON THE SUN! .......... 102

NO MORE DISCOUNTS...YOU DESERVE THE BEST! .......... 107

BLACK SELF-CARE! "BLACK LOVE, BLACK SOLIDARITY, AND BLACK COMMUNITY COMPASSION". .......... 111

ABOUT THE AUTHOR .......... 121

# Intro

Good Vibes is a collection of positive energies in written form. Originating from the Good Vibes with Dr. S blog, I wanted to provide a space where you can have all the energy and good vibrations under one positive roof so to speak. Every entry provides an opportunity to experience a positive spark of thought, perspective, and reflection. There is power within us all to experience good energy. We must increase our capacity to receive that energy by broadening our horizons, releasing what no longer serves us, and lastly allowing what strengths us to flow continuously. Good Vibes does not mean that we will never encounter Bad Vibes, it just means that we can shift our mood and create the vibes we desire. There is power in our ability to choose and we must decide that there is always an opportunity to grow from whatever we have experienced. The positive times teach us gratitude and appreciation. The tough times teach us patience, resilience, and allow for recognition of our own strengths. We often do not realize where our behaviors originate. There is an opportunity to explore deeper by reading this book and doing some self-reflecting in the process. I want this book to provoke enlightenment, which is different from your standard self-improvement books, which provide for you, "The Blueprint for Success" or information on "How to Change Your Life in 10 days". This book is centered on discovery and exploration of self. As you read the Good Vibes entries, I want you to ask questions of yourself. This book does not require you to know all the answers. What I am requesting of you is that you promise yourself that you will continue to explore various parts of your existence. The journey does not require us to be hyper-focused on the destination but to realize that there are mini destinations within our travels to appreciate and enjoy. Those are the Good Vibes. Those are the moments of happiness, reflection, and growth that I hope this book provides for you. So, let us take this trip! Good Vibes with Dr. S

Enjoy!

# Do not Rob Yourself of Peace, by Living with Regrets.

It is never easy to accept that maybe we have made some wrong choices in our lives. I mean who has not looked back at least once and said, I should have done things differently? This way of processing makes us human and happens so often that we may not even notice it. It is also not the thief I am referring to in the title of this post. That perpetrator is much more sinister than a simple act of occasional reflection. Regrets are like armed robbers of our peace. They invade our mental spaces in search of any instance of joy that we are currently experiencing. Regret has no compassion for us or the timing in which it will arrive to mess with our happiness. If we fail to defend our mental and emotional safes of peace and joy, Regret will surely remove them from us. So, how does it happen?

**Regret is defined by deep sadness or disappointment that is triggered by something in our past. This may be a loss, missed opportunity, or decision we may have made.** It literally disrupts our present functioning, even if we are Happy, Content, and in a place of Peace. Why do we allow Regrets to creep back in and take away what we have worked so hard to get back into our lives? For many of us, it has been a battle to reach a point of saying, "Okay, now I'm fine" or to declare, "I'm not letting anyone steal my joy anymore"! We say it with such confidence, and I believe most people truly mean it. You are not allowing anyone to come and confiscate your peace. You stand strong against the toxic ways of people and have even cut people off who have continuously targeted your treasures of Peace and Happiness. **There is no doubt you are strong when it comes to the enemy you can see but Regret is sneaky, calculating, and cunning.** It enters your surroundings mentally with just one thought. It utilizes surveillance to closely monitor your mental and emotional health…soon as there is one moment of disappointment in your current life, Regret strikes with an onslaught of negative thoughts from your past. Regrets utilize your current moments of vulnerability to bring past pain, disappointments, and hurts to the surface. It bets on the power of the mind to go back in time and bring things from our past into our present.

**Regret moves us to be like an old well that has a deep hole into the ground (our thoughts). The well also has a basket, long rope, and a turning device that allows us to lower it deep into the depths for water (suppressed thoughts).** Regrets push us to the point where we lower that basket all the way to the bottom (our past) and bring everything to the top (conscious thoughts). So of course, we are triggered by the things in our baskets. Opportunities that did not work out, relationships that may have failed, Memories of people we have loss, and past pain. Regrets are evil disrupters of Happiness and Joy. Regrets are not Reflections. Reflecting is a positive action where we go back in time briefly, typically to see how far we have traveled or to put things in perspective. As always, let us talk about how we can reclaim, respond, and reset when Regrets strike against us. Let us arm ourselves so we are prepared if attacked again by Regrets. Yes, we will be attacked again!

Let us remember that Regrets disrupt our present by triggering us mentally and emotionally about things in our past. **Often in life, we simply move on from things in our past. Just by the very nature of time continuing and often because we believe that we have healed from that thing that Regret attaches to with a firm grip.** Many times, we have not fully resolved the issue and often we simply suppress it because we must move on, Right? Whatever it was, caused us some major pain during that time and we had to escape it to just go on with life. Work did not stop, school did not stop, and so on. The world continued spinning and I needed to spin with it or find myself stuck in that very anxiety provoking and scary space. Although, we may have moved on physically...mentally and emotionally we may still have some attachment to that event, person, or thing. **Regret would not target something or someone you do not have any attachment to because you would not be triggered by insignificant things.** Some people believe we can just Let Go of things and people from our past. I believe it is extremely easy to say and more challenging to execute. What I do believe we have the power to do is Attach Peace to anything from our past. The reason Regret aims at your Peace is because it knows that Peace is the Power you must kill all regrets.

It is never easy to accept that maybe we have made some wrong choices in our lives. I mean who has not looked back at least once and said, I should have done things differently? This way of processing makes us human and happens so often that we may not even notice it. It is also not the thief I am referring to in the title of this post. That perpetrator is much more sinister than a simple act of occasional reflection. Regrets are like armed robbers of our peace. They invade our mental spaces in search of any instance of joy that we are currently experiencing. Regret has no compassion for us or the timing in which it will arrive to mess with our happiness. If we fail to defend our mental and emotional safes of peace and joy, Regret will surely remove them from us. So, how does it happen?

**Regret is defined by deep sadness or disappointment that is triggered by something in our past. This may be a loss, missed opportunity, or decision we may have made.** It literally disrupts our present functioning, even if we are Happy, Content, and in a place of Peace. Why do we allow Regrets to creep back in and take away what we have worked so hard to get back into our lives? For many of us, it has been a battle to reach a point of saying, "Okay, now I'm fine" or to declare, "I'm not letting anyone steal my joy anymore"! We say it with such confidence, and I believe most people truly mean it. You are not allowing anyone to come and confiscate your peace. You stand strong against the toxic ways of people and have even cut people off who have continuously targeted your treasures of Peace and Happiness. **There is no doubt you are strong when it comes to the enemy you can see but Regret is sneaky, calculating, and cunning.** It enters your surroundings mentally with just one thought. It utilizes surveillance to closely monitor your mental and emotional health…soon as there is one moment of disappointment in your current life, Regret strikes with an onslaught of negative thoughts from your past. Regrets utilize your current moments of vulnerability to bring past pain, disappointments, and hurts to the surface. It bets on the power of the mind to go back in time and bring things from our past into our present.

**Regret moves us to be like an old well that has a deep hole into the ground (our thoughts). The well also has a basket, long rope, and a turning device that allows us to lower it deep into the depths for water (suppressed thoughts).** Regrets push us to the point where we lower that basket all the way to the bottom (our past) and bring everything to the top (conscious thoughts). So of course, we are triggered by the things in our baskets. Opportunities that did not work out, relationships that may have failed, Memories of people we have loss, and past pain. Regrets are evil disrupters of Happiness and Joy. Regrets are not Reflections. Reflecting is a positive action where we go back in time briefly, typically to see how far we have traveled or to put things in perspective. As always, let us talk about how we can reclaim, respond, and reset when Regrets strike against us. Let us arm ourselves so we are prepared if attacked again by Regrets. Yes, we will be attacked again!

Let us remember that Regrets disrupt our present by triggering us mentally and emotionally about things in our past. **Often in life, we simply move on from things in our past. Just by the very nature of time continuing and often**

**because we believe that we have healed from that thing that Regret attaches to with a firm grip.** Many times, we have not fully resolved the issue and often we simply suppress it because we must move on, Right? Whatever it was, caused us some major pain during that time and we had to escape it to just go on with life. Work did not stop, school did not stop, and so on. The world continued spinning and I needed to spin with it or find myself stuck in that very anxiety provoking and scary space. Although, we may have moved on physically…mentally and emotionally we may still have some attachment to that event, person, or thing. **Regret would not target something or someone you do not have any attachment to because you would not be triggered by insignificant things.** Some people believe we can just Let Go of things and people from our past. I believe that is extremely easy to say and more challenging to execute. What I do believe we have the power to do is Attach Peace to anything from our past. The reason Regret aims at your Peace is because it knows that Peace is the Power you must kill all regrets.

**To truly Heal from something in our past is to have Peace with it. Last time I checked, there are no time machines that will allow us to physically go back to the past but Our Minds (The Well) can allow us to go back in time to make Peace with that thing.** We have the power to go back mentally and emotionally in time and close chapters in our lives that were left open. We can do it mentally and I have a few exercises, which may help you with that process. I want you to make a list of anything from your past that still bothers you when Regret strikes. If you're ready to close that chapter (Therapy can help with this part as well), I want you to cross it off the list and write, "I'm at Peace with This" next to it. **Now what you are doing is mentally closing books, vulnerable spots, healing old wounds, and resolving past discomforts.** Sounds too easy. It really does and I do not believe it will necessarily be for some people, but it will be worth it for sure. **Another exercise that I believe will benefit you even more, is to simply make Peace a part of your daily life. Make Peace the metaphoric armor that surrounds you and protects you against Regret.** Where there's Peace, Regret cannot enter. If we make Peace who we are and Seeking Peace one of Our Life's Goals…we will be more prepared when Regret strikes again. Walking in Peace does not guarantee that Regret will not attempt to find dents in our armor, but it does provide our greatest overall protection when faced with the challenge. Write down a few things that bring you Peace and keep that list near. When challenged by Regrets, read that list. You will immediately begin to dis-empower Regrets and they will Retreat from your life.

**Peace is our greatest weapon against Regret. Stay armed by simply seeking peace and protecting yours at all cost. Peace is Protection.**

Good Vibes!

- **Peace is a powerful asset to our everyday functioning. It allows us to be grounded during challenging times.**
- **Regrets can lead to Resentment. It is okay to turn the page and continue writing.**
- **I know you want to look back but look at all you must be grateful for in the present.**

**Good Thoughts:**

# Prioritizing Me! A Commitment to My Self-Care.

**I am sure you can tell by the title of this post that this is another one of those Self-Care is vital and paramount to my overall wellness post.** Well, you are both right and wrong. Right because this post is about the importance of self-care and why you should make it a necessary aspect of your daily life. Wrong, because this is not just another one of those posts in that I am not writing to preach, condemn, or make you feel bad about not making time for yourself. This post is so much more than that. This is written to be a lasting declaration, a pledge like no other, and a commitment that you will from here on out…Make You The Priority.

It is okay if this has not been your attitude prior to reading this post. **Just a little reminder that since the beginning of your existence, you have been conditioned to make yourself anything but the priority in your life.** In every aspect of our society, we have asked individuals to put people, places, and ideas before themselves in order of importance. So, it is no wonder why you struggle to be consistent in your Self-Care habits and behaviors. Of course, you always approach a new self-care regiment with good intentions and may even experience fleeting moments of success. You let others know with confidence that this is the new you and they better get used to you saying, "No" to anything that is not aligned with you taking care of you. I love it. I think it is great that you have attempted to change the game for yourself and finally decided that you deserve the peace that comes with self-care. How is it going? Does it seem like you are on a roller coaster of a ride when it comes to making yourself **The Priority**?

I want to make a particularly important distinction between making yourself "A Priority" and making yourself "The Priority". Making yourself a priority, means that there are other priorities on the same level as you. Although, very compassionate and caring of you…**I am sincerely requesting that you make yourself, "THE PRIORITY"! (This is a shift in thinking that is needed to break the cycle).** Is it even realistic you ask? Is it possible that I could come before my partner, my kids, my job, school, and anything else that I am leaving out? Yes! I do believe it is realistic, doable, and sustainable. I also do not believe it is as difficult as we make it out to be. Even with the powerful forces of conditioning, there is a way to break away from the invisible constraints and anti-self-care narratives that you have been written into against your will. Often, without you even realizing it. **How does one free themselves from "invisible" cages or remove themselves from "false" narratives? It is simple if you think about it. If the cages are invisible and the narratives are false, do they even exist?** I would say with confidence, No. So why does it seem so difficult to break away from what is both invisible and false? Well, the string pullers or powers that be have injected false-truths and invisible bars into your psyche and have also constructed actual systems to perpetuate these enemies to your self-care.

**You only have to look at work hours, societal expectations, gender roles, religion, school, the concept of time, and more as variables that reinforce the idea that you can never be, *Thee Priority*.** So, breaking away from this very anti-prioritizing script is both a simple and complex task that you must commit to. It is simple in that what does not exist and what is not true, no longer has to keep you in bondage. It is also complex because you are expected to move and are functioning within the current elements in our society. The same elements you and others have made a part of your journey since your very first step will make the process challenging. **What is life without a challenge or two? Although dealing with these life variables are inherently**

**difficult, I believe people struggle with the invisible cages and false narratives more than anything else.** It is often what you cannot see that will bring you the most difficulty in making yourself the priority. There is an enormous amount of mental strain that takes place in the process of becoming the priority. There is an internal conflict between being the priority and guilt for not putting others/other things first. It just does not seem right to write your name at the top of that priority list. Even when you write your name at the top, you struggle to refrain from erasing it or crossing it out. It is just the power that has been woven into the false narrative that Self-Care is Selfish. Who wants to be considered selfish? **Even internal feelings of selfishness are enough to not only cross yourself out of the pole position of your priority list, you will feel so bad that you are okay with making yourself 10th on the list just to make sure.** Declare today, **NO MORE!**

It is time to get to work. ***I would like you to make an actual Priority List.*** I want you to ***write the word, ME at the top of that list***. You can follow ME with anyone or anything you choose. ***Now, I want you to write 5 or more reasons why you deserve to be The Priority.*** This is important because not only do you have an actual Priority List with You at the top, you are now constructing mental support beams to hold up this new construct you are developing and building. Here is another important step. ***I want you to fill as many spaces of your life with these words…I AM THE PRIORITY!*** Write it on things in your home, use post it notes and keep them in your car. ***Utilize your phone to create voice reminders that you can play anytime you are compelled to cross out or erase, "ME" from the TOP POSITION on your Priority List.*** Here is another important step. ***Write down a list of self-care activities and declarations that prove you are truly The Priority.*** Some examples are the following: "I will Say No when I want", "I will take time for ME", Exercise, Quiet time, Solo getaways, and anything else you determine to bring you Happiness and Joy.

Lastly, I just want you to Commit! Make a commitment to yourself first and then those you love. **Become the very embodiment of Self-Care. So much so that there is no separation between you and caring for yourself.** You ARE CARING FOR YOURSELF and aligned with the phrase in every aspect. You are not only freeing yourself from the invisible cage, you are writing yourself out of the false narrative that you will never be the Priority. You are unlearning all the negative learned behavior that has placed you 2nd, 3rd, 7th, and 20th on the Priority List. Starting immediately, you are declaring with confidence and unwavering intention, **I AM PRIORITIZING ME! I AM MAKING A**

COMMITMENT to MY SELF-CARE for me and those I love. Declare, I WILL NO LONGER POUR FROM AN EMPTY CUP. I WILL BE FULL FROM THIS DAY FORWARD!

Commit to reading this whenever you need a reminder. YOU GOT THIS!

Good Vibes!

- Self-Care is whatever you need it to be. Whatever restores you in your self-care.
- You deserve to be the priority. It is up to you to ensure that you come first.
- Get Confident with your "No"! It just may save your life.

**Good Thoughts:**

# I am Cool with Change. It is the Changing Part that's Tough for Me.

**It seems like every day, I come across a caption or a post about how we cannot stay the same once this Covid-19 thing is over.** How returning to who we were before would be some sort of sign that we have failed or missed an opportunity to grow or evolve. Listen, as someone who has worked with people on the idea and concept of Change for over 20 years…not even a Global Pandemic can force people to Change if they are not ready. The reason being is that Change is still one of the most challenging, difficult, exciting, uncomfortable, and rewarding processes that can occur in our lives. So, why is it still the most resistant and anxiety provoking thing for so many of us? The answer may be found in our individual capacities to Change but also in Our easiness and comfort in staying the same. Why move from this seemingly delusional state of comfortability? **The internal dialogue of, "Nope, not changing…I'm good here. Thanks", will have**

**us Cool with Change but Resistant to Changing. That is not only difficult to accept, it may also be the reason we are continuously falling short in many areas of our lives.**

**The fundamental process of Change was never intended to be easy in the sense that any movement away from what has been normal will require adjustment, re-calibration, and re-configuring.** As we are disrupted from our cozy spaces, we either grab on to something to keep us grounded in what is comfortable or we resist the change because, ideally this is where we want to remain. Although, I have never experienced a major earthquake, I would believe that as the earth is shaking and moving us that we would quickly seek shelter (safety) and/or grab on to something secure (stability). Our resistance to change has to do with the safety of what is comfortable, the stability of what's comfortable, and fear of the unknown. What may be on the Horizon is not worth risking what is presently known. So, it seems…so we rather stay where we are. I am cool with you guys changing, all for your family/friends changing, but as for me…nah I'm good here. Carry on with post Covid-19 Change Talk, I will just see what happens. Using the Power of Flow, that language of "let's just see what happens" would be more than acceptable. I would argue that it's probably your greatest ally in truly accepting change but typically **"let's just see what happens" is avoidance language and rooted in the idea of**

**waiting rather than the idea of faith, which requires both Belief and Work. To just see what happens is not faith or manifesting.** Although change is constant…swimming with against the current of change can prove to be exhausting and dangerous. There's work to be done, even in Changing.

I am sure you have noticed by now that Expressing that You are Changing is the wave. I am cutting people off, getting rid of toxic behaviors, starting that new endeavor, Healing, and Growing. **The only problem is that if Expressing Change is the Wave than Actually Changing is the solid Rock of a Mountain that seems insurmountable and impenetrable.** As a result, when faced with the actual process of changing, we allow the Mountain to Win. ***If we are all Changing, why are we Repeating? Let us think about this. If we are changing and not just expressing change, why are we continuously falling in the same holes, for the same people, the same challenges, and into the same situations…repeatedly?*** I know, "Dr. S but we are human, we're going to stumble sometimes". That is a fact! But if you are stumbling for the 789th time over the same pebble…that is not stumbling. That is being comfortable with your fall, expecting your fall, and in some cases…starting your fall before you begin to fall. That is not change at all but as always, it is not my intention or plan to give the problem of changing the limelight in this post. The final scene, the star of the show, and the primary focus must be on the Solution to resisting change and changing.

Just like all my previous posts, I do not have a magic pill or potion to remedy the resistance to actual changing condition that has impacted our society. I do not have the vaccine to why we keep repeating the same negative behaviors repeatedly. I don't have the cure for why we have gotten so comfortable with our political figures that we just blindly follow, accept, and vote for political parties without actually holding them accountable for actually changing things instead of expressing that this will be the year of change. **I do have a solution. You! You are your greatest answer, solution, strategy for resolving any challenges you are having around not only expressing change but changing. I Really Believe In You! It is time that You Believe in You!**

You are resistant to changing because where you are is safe, stable, comfortable, and free of fear. Why would you change that, right? **Well, what if I told you that this space you are currently in is not actually any of those things. If it were safe, why would repeatedly be hurt or in pain in that space? If it was stable, why are you always mentally and emotionally moving around? If it is comfortable, why are you stressing, anxious, or worried? Lastly, if it is free of fear…why are you afraid of what is to come?** The reason being is that by the very nature of staying in the same place, our minds create a pseudo shelter of safety because we have cognitively created it in order to fit the reality we want to have in front of us. We have constructed what we believe to what is best for us because it does not require any movement, hard truth telling, or self-evaluation. It does not test our ego, or the perception others may have of us. It is easy to stay here…so we say. As we continue to fall short. It is time to actually change!

Stop fighting change. Easy concept to consider. **Instead of Fighting, Flow. Be fluid and allow change to carry you to where you need to be and where you want to be. I am safety, I am stability, I am okay in discomfort, and I am fearless. The unknown is beautiful. The discomfort is part of the process of growing.** I can Flow because I know that life is fluid. Change is the Only Thing that is Constant on This Journey. If I am fluid and allow flow to take place…I will move with Change. I will trust the process of Change because wherever I am carried to is where I need to be. I am excited for what is on the other side of my change. I am motivated by the idea of change so I will seek opportunities to be uncomfortable, to be in places I once feared, to go where it's not "so safe", and to be where it may not be "so stable". If I believe in myself, I can climb the insurmountable mountain of changing and see what is on the other side. Read this last section repeatedly as you change. Let this be a reminder that to simple express change is not enough. **To Actually Change means that I Am More than Enough…to reach my goals, overcome the challenges of changing, and to get to the other side.**

**Keep Changing!**

**Good Vibes!**

- **Change is never easy but even small steps can build motivation. Baby steps!**
- **Change may feel uncomfortable at first but that is the process of preparing you.**
- **Just know that no matter the change that comes your way, you will be fine.**

**Good Thoughts:**

# Forget Outside, There's Inside Work to Do!

**There is a rush to head back outside and get back to all the exciting activities. People are missing that world we called normal and it is even culturally significant in Hip-Hop to state with confidence, "I'm Outside"!** It really makes me wonder…are many of us looking to hurry up and get outside to avoid the overdue work that needs to take place inside. I am talking about resolving, repairing, and resetting from within. This pandemic has sat many of us down and forced us to be inside of ourselves. Many of us have used this time to self-reflect and self-evaluate. We knew that we were avoiding the work of doing an internal assessment of where we are on our journey. **It was so easy to allow ourselves to be consumed by outside forces of social interactions, work, and a seemingly never-ending state of busyness….But Now,**

**things have shifted for many of us, Inside is the only place to go.**

**I believe this pandemic may be a blessing in disguise. As crazy as that sounds, a sudden and unexpected shift in what we considered to be normal has moved us to reconsider so many things.** How we take care of ourselves, how we take care of others, and where do we go from here? Also, many of us were running on "E", still making it happen but barely. Those fumes allowed us to continue caring for others, meet our deadlines, and somehow squeeze in some moments of "me" time. We made it through another week, with an exhale of "I'm not sure how I got here". I want you to know that our mind and bodies are so powerful that they can run on autopilot, even if it is truly not what is best for us…. We just stay on go. **It is amazing how much we can endure when we have been conditioned to do so. We will literally overlook our inner selves to ensure that the world around us is filled with all it needs. It is fine because now is the perfect time to begin your journey of intentional inner work.**

**Some areas are already opening and that is fine because "Inside Work" does not move according to the principles and policies of the Outside.** That means even though there is a re-opening on the outside, there can be a Grand Reopening on the Inside. A reviving of your inner self that can mean different things to different people. For some it may be healing, recharging, or resting. For others it may be revamping, detoxing, and reinventing. Honestly, it does not matter what you call it if you are looking inward for some form of growth and strength. **The outside is not always our friend. In fact, the "outside" may be the reason many of us are not achieving the level of peace we desire. Too much time "Outside" can block blessings, slow healing, and trigger new wounds.** I am using the word, "Outside" in two ways. The literal since of the word, outside as a physical space away from what we call home. That would be our work, day parties, school, religious gatherings, etc.... **I am also referring to "Outside" in a metaphorical sense as external worries, conditions, expectations, narratives, social media, and so on. So often we give power to those outside of us by over valuing their opinions and allowing people to write our stories without our consent.** Why are we so drawn by outside forces? Sometimes it seems that we rather escape "Our Inside" so bad that we haphazardly accept any energy that comes our way from the Outside. I wonder if we truly understood the internal jewelry we possess, if we would so freely disregard it for the possibilities of what the outside may bring us. **There is a work inside of you that can unlock so many blessings, wisdom, and over-standing. The challenge is to stop fighting against the work within you**

**and to allow the flow inward to take place free of external constraints designed to keep you outside.**

**How do we begin to make Inside Work a consistent part of our lives? I believe it all starts with an intentional desire and motivation to Stay Inside.** That is only the beginning of this work as the doing is most often the most difficult part. Surely, the distractions will undoubtedly move to interfere and stop you from reaching the deepest parts of you. Instead of shifting your focus on stopping the distractions, increase your focus on the inner work. Here are a few ideas to begin to do some "Inside Work". Move into a space of peace. **Quiet your mind by thinking calming thoughts and meditating on internal silence. Start with simple declarations of release, "I release anything that keeps me bound". Also try, "I am free from the opinions and expectations of others". You can also begin to do some self-exploration. Questions such as, "Who Am I"? or 'Why Am I Here"?** Other action steps may move you to begin to process past hurts, traumas, or experiences that have led to patterns of negative behaviors and coping strategies that damage your internal wiring. There is of course an opportunity to begin Therapy, but it is important to realize that your therapist can not do the "Inside Work" for you. **They can guide you, encourage you, and empower you towards the depths of your core but they can only go but so far. If its**

**healing you desire, do the "Inside Work". If it is growth you desire, do the "Inside Work".**

**Just know that as the world rushes to get back outside, there will be some of us who rush to "Stay Inside".** We realize that there is more work to do and this enlightening experience can propel us to new levels. An experience that we can no longer avoid or ignore. What is inside of us must be worked on and cultivated. **What is inside of us may unlock something new and that will bring us outside in a brand-new way.** Outside with confidence, alignment, and wholeness. This is the season to Stay Inside…. may you discover You within You.

**Be Well!**

**Good Vibes!**

- **What is inside of you that requires your compassion and love?**
- **Have you been neglecting some things on the inside? Let us explore areas that need your attention.**
- **This is the perfect time to love yourself unconditionally. Write down some ways you can focus on you during this season.**

**Good Thoughts:**

# Do not Walk Away from Your Purpose!

**It is easy to understand why so many people feel like, it is not even worth it anymore to follow their dreams.** Some people may be even questioning their purpose as so many other things seem more important right now. Talk about a crazy year, how do we even put it into words? How would you describe 2020? Some may use adjectives like sad, depressing, a roller coaster ride, a scary movie, or simply…indescribable. Many people are questioning their own place in this new normal as many people call it. There is a rush to pivot approaches, adapt to technology, and recreate ourselves to fit the current times that we are living. For some that may be easy to do and for others, it can be extremely challenging. It is not that those individuals are not talented, creative, or resilient. It is just the idea and actuality of adjusting can be really overwhelming. **I believe there is a way to make the transition a little easier…focus on Your Purpose not Your Pivot!**

When our energy is predominantly focused on changing it up or re-branding, there is a good chance we may lose sight of it all. Not to mention the enormity of having to restructure what we believed was our goldmine of an idea. **Our eyes were set on bringing something special to the world and 2020 has quickly reminded us that not everything is in our control.** But wait…Our Purpose is not controlled, manipulated, or dictated by outside forces. It does not exist in a state in which external forces can end it, take it away, or lessen its power. **Your Purpose is divine. Something greater than even that of a Pandemic. Covid-19 cannot end your purpose!** This Pandemic may Reveal Your Purpose. You may have started to experience a sense of clarity because of all that has taken place this year. **So, although there may be a thought of abandoning a dream or some amazing idea…those things are not always aligned with Purpose. Those are tools that help build Purpose, but the Rock will always be Your Purpose.**

**YOU ARE PURPOSE!** To walk away from Your Purpose is to Walk Away from You. So many people will ask me, "Doc, how do I find my Purpose? What is it? I'm just not sure'! Although my answer may not be as hyper-revealing or cosmically powerful as they would like…it is still pretty telling. **Your Purpose is Inside of You. You just need to keep Exploring.** I often think we see Purpose Exploration the way we seek out something of value when we go shopping. For example, we head out to the store in search for the perfect item and when we find it, there is a rush of joy. That tangible thing creates a surge of happiness because we can touch it, see it, and in its physical form a physiological reaction takes place. We did it! **This what we often believe the "Finding of Our Purpose" will be like and it is no wonder we are often disappointed when this is not the experience at all. What we often encounter are feelings of emptiness, decreased self-worth, insecurities, and questions.**

Why has everyone else found their purpose but I have no idea? **How did they experience their "aha moment" and I'm stuck with countless "ah nah" moments? One of the most mentally dangerous things you can do is to equate the visible happiness, fun times, and "I love what I do" Instagram expressions with people living in purpose.** Even more important, why does it even matter in the overall context of you seeking Your Purpose? It does not!!! **What is for You will Only Be for You! If that does not bring you a sense of peace, I do not know what else will.** In other words, Your Purpose will Never Escape You! That is why Purpose itself is Peace. Once you are fully committed to being aligned with Your Purpose, a sense of calm will come over you because it is yours! This does not mean that becoming one with your Purpose does not bring on feelings of anxiousness or doubt at times because it does…more than you can imagine. **What I will say is that Purpose allows us to return to it, when we need to be grounded during the storms of life. It has a comforting way of reassuring, "I'll be fine".**

So, the title of the blog post is kind of misleading. **Do not Walk Away from Your Purpose! It is stated with strength, almost like a commandment of sort.** It is not possible at all (well maybe not possible). See, to walk away from your purpose is to walk away from yourself. People would have to try hard to walk away from their purpose and the walking away is typically a Mental process. **Even in those feelings of uncertainty and emptiness, Purpose is always Present.** It is like having a precious diamond in your possession and being so distracted or overly consumed by the chaos of the world, you forget you have it. **It is not about the monetary value of the diamond because contrary to what many believe, Purpose does not always align with Monetary Riches.** The value of the diamond is better defined as Peace, Comfort, and Security. **That is the Real Wealth of Purpose!**

**You can walk away from your purpose when you can walk away from your shadow. Purpose is even more powerful than that example because shade may hide your shadow to your physical eye, but Purpose is found within the wiring of your soul.** What you seek to do is to find the tools, vehicles, or mediums to bring life to your purpose. ***Your stress is not with finding your purpose, it is with finding the means to give your purpose metaphoric legs to walk and do.*** Just do not focus on the tools to say to the world, "Look world, I have a purpose…or I'm living my purpose"! One, it does not matter and Two, Purpose is felt so it does not matter! You do not have to say a word. Does that make sense? **If you are your purpose and you have the physiological tools of hands, feet, a brain, and so on…the only thing left is to Just Do it!**

**Do not Walk Away from Your Purpose! Walk with It! It will never leave you!**
**Good Vibes!**

- **Purpose is present in exploration, discovery, and discomfort. Seek and You will find!**
- **Your Purpose does not have an expiration date. So, you do not have to rush.**
- **Stop looking for your purpose in the comparisons of others. What is for you, is yours!**

**Good Thoughts:**

# Keep Your Apologies...Change Your Behavior!

**We are an apology crazed society that loves to robotically utter the words, "I'm sorry" whenever we are guilty of doing wrong to others.** I am not talking about people with those occasional blunders that we are all guilty of doing. I am talking about the repeat offenders that seem to have an, "I'm sorry" button attached to them that automatically activates whenever their confronted about their act of wrongdoing. You know the real reason we have come to accept apologies so easily? **We have created in our minds the image of who we want the perpetrator of wrong to be instead of coming to terms with the reality in front of us..." this person may have some issues"!**

On the other end, it is a lack of accountability that has permeated the internal wiring of many people. **It is almost**

**insulting to them that we demand accountability from them. How dare you hold me accountable for what I have done. Why do not you simply take this apology in exchange for letting me off the hook again for the 99,000th time.** I already said I am sorry and he or she knows that if that "I'm sorry" is coupled with an, "I promise" …it is a wrap! You can in many cases just throw accountability out the window. So, here is, the question…. why are we so scared to challenge and confront these individuals? **Why is it difficult for us to push the accountability button and hold people to a certain standard regarding how they treat us? The answers are in the power of an apology.**

An apology is like sending out front line soldiers in a conflict. It softens the initial defense systems within us. It decreases the emotions of anger and frustration while increasing our patience. Our tolerance levels become elevated and we often, simply concede. **That's right, you fell for it again. Remember you said this time you would be tough? You said you would hold them accountable…you said, "I'm done"! Yeah right. Here you are again, just accepting another apology with hopes of changed behavior showing up at some point in time.** I want you to be mindful of this important point related to why some of us accept apologies so readily than others. **Our personal**

**experiences, some dating back to our childhood may contribute to the why in our struggles with both accepting apologies and/or not holding people accountable. Many of us innately see the good in people.** Meaning, we see their mishaps as slip-ups in moments of time versus real representation of their true character.

**Let us not forget that there are people in abusive and toxic relationships that accept apologies because of the mental control and emotional tricks of their abusers and perpetrators.** We know that ***apologies and "promises" of change can be weapons of manipulation*** by those who seek to suppress real change to continue their ability to control their victims. Listen, I get it. None of this stuff is easy to resolve due to the complexities of being humans with layers filled with desires of happiness, hopes, past trauma, fantasies of forever love, and expectations of loyalty as well as empathy. Bottom line…it's complicated! Never blame yourself for how others mistreat you. Do not engage in self-destructive and self-abusive behaviors because of the ill-intentions of others. **This is not a post to tear down anyone. I am not interested in making those like myself who have accepted apologies easily throughout my life, feel bad about those decisions. I also see the human side of the toxic and abusive individual.** I understand that there are many underlying reasons why people may behave the way they do. So, what do we do about it?

**I believe we can start by letting people keep their apologies and demand that people change their behavior.** Makes sense, right? If people are committed to the relationship, partnership, or connection…it shouldn't be difficult, right? I know many will ask, "Dr. S, how can we demand someone change their behavior"? **The word demand seems so harsh…very confrontational. Exactly! A person who utilizes apologies in a way to escape change will certainty not want any demands of accountability to be discussed but that is what needs to take place.** It challenges the behavior and can be empowering for you as you confidently demand behavior shifts over nice and kindly worded apologies.

**So, when should we begin to expect changed behavior over an apology? Immediately after the first offense!** We can be patient, tolerant, empathetic, and strong in holding others accountable for their actions. **Please do not think that I do not see the value in apologizing…I do! I just believe changed behavior holds more weight.** If we can collectively but more so individually become more focused on Accountability over Apologizing, we will make changed behavior the new norm. **Bottom line…Keep Your Apology and turn it into Changed Behavior.**

**Let us see if expectation becomes reality…demand it!**

**Good Vibes!**

**Good Thoughts:**

# We all need some R & R! "Relationship Reciprocity".

It has always been said that one of the most important factors in a successful relationship is communication. I agree with this 100%. Communication is **ONE** of the most important factors in relationship success but it's not the only thing that determines whether you ride into the sunset with your partner or are throwing their clothes out the window, yelling "Get Out"! This blog post is about R & R and NO, I am not talking about rest and relaxation…something I am sure all of us could use a little more of right about now. **I am talking about Relationship Reciprocity. You know, that matching of whatever we bring into our sacred connection.** It is that alignment of energy, appreciation, support, love, and encouragement that makes us feel something special about nurturing our relationship. The Soulful Hip-Hop Goddess, Lauryn Hill made it a relationship standard question when she said, "Tell me, who I have to be…To get some reciprocity"? **Her wording was powerful in that she was questioning whether she needed to become someone else to obtain something so valuable as reciprocity.** She spoke eloquently about this fundamental need to have your partner reciprocate if we were going to expect our union to grow and ascend.

**The word Reciprocity has to do with an exchange of things, I also like to include energies, vibes, resources, and more for mutual benefit.** Since the beginning of time, Reciprocity has come to be an expectation in any relationship. Over time, has this expectation been diluted by the quote, "Expect Nothing, Accept Everything"? I believe the quote is absolutely true but as with many things in today's vernacular, context needs to be considered because it matters. That quote is seemingly used to decreased distress and anxiety related to things beyond our control. It allows us to be calm during moments of distress by accepting in total, all that has come to us without expectation of what will happen next. I am not sure this should apply to Reciprocity. **It seems that Reciprocity is not only something to wish for in a relationship, IT IS THE RELATIONSHIP!** Reciprocity is harmony but not that perfect utopias or "Me and my boo never argue" harmony that many people like to portray in their relationships. When I talk about Reciprocity being harmony, I am speaking about an Exchange of Understanding. **That is my partner**

**reciprocates with an effort to understand who I am and I in exchange provide the same in return.** Another way of seeing the connection between Reciprocity and Harmony is to explore the true way of resolving any discord. It is not about a win-win or a win-lose. It is all about reaching a place of Understanding where one tries to see beyond the imperfections, disagreements of perspective, or words. **Without that Understanding or Reciprocity, how can a relationship expect to thrive? In other words, a relationship that is empty of Reciprocity is simply put, Surviving or Hanging On. The lack of Reciprocity will leave your Relationship fragile and unable to withstand the tough times, ALL relationships will encounter.** Feelings of emotional inequality, loneliness, and feeling unappreciated can all develop from a lack of reciprocity.

It does not matter what needs to be mutually exchanged in a relationship, if it is not Reciprocated…unhappiness will be cultivated. The easiest example to discuss is that of finances. I have seen plenty of questions posed like this, "Would you be with someone who makes $25,000 a year if you make $100,000 a year"? Again, this example is not about Reciprocity as there is not full context provided in the question. ***If there is Reciprocity or Understanding in the relationship, there is nothing to say that this example could not be a successful relationship.*** Remember, I am talking about harmony on a deeper level. Although, some may argue that finances are everything in a relationship, it also depends on what is valued. **What I mean by this, using the same example above is that a person who makes $25,000 a year can Reciprocate something else that is mutually beneficial to their partner that makes $100,000 year because there is an understanding of what's valuable and needed by the other person.** It may not be money at all. This same principle of Reciprocity can be applied to any aspect of a relationship. That includes finances, sex, emotional health, attention, and so many other variables that are considered important aspects of a successful relationship.

**As a Mental-Health Therapist, I do need to speak on the connection between Lack of Reciprocity in Relationships and symptoms of Depression, Anxiety, and Decreased Self-Worth.** Everyone will scream it; YOU CAN'T DEPEND ON SOMEONE ELSE TO MAKE YOU HAPPY! ***Can we be real and transparent? People who expect Reciprocity in a relationship are not always depending on the other person to Make Them Happy.*** Reciprocation is a process that is tied to self-care. If I continually pour from my cup into yours, my cup should also stay full, as your overflow will refill my cup again and again. Should I depend on you to refill my cup? No, but should I expect a level of understanding that my cup desires to be refilled to some extent by you? Yes! When this does not occur, one can begin to feel tired in the relationship. **The person may also experience symptoms of Depression as the physical and emotional exhaustion of pouring all one has into someone without some level of Reciprocity or Understanding can be too much to take.** Anxiety can develop from a lack of Reciprocity as one becomes hyper-fixated on the why. Why is my partner not reciprocating in some form? **A person may start overthinking the lack of understanding, being overly present in moments of discord, and lastly...questioning their own self-worth.** Self-esteem issues can begin to arise as well from a lack of Relationship Reciprocity. **A person may begin to ask themselves, "Am I not good enough"? "Is there something I'm doing wrong"? "Does my partner not find me important enough to provide me with that Reciprocity"?** Let me remind you of how Lauryn Hill started that famous bar, "Tell me who I have to be". **One may feel like they can no longer be themselves, triggering self-concept issues to find the Reciprocity they so intensely desire.** Do not be discouraged if Reciprocity is decreasing or nonexistent in your relationship. There's hope!

So as always, I like to speak about solutions in my blog post. **Sometimes I list possible solutions and other times, my suggested solution is simply enlightenment.** Meaning, you must explore what Relationship Reciprocation means to you and how seeking a level of understanding from your partner can be vital to a thriving relationship. I will of course suggest this one simple but especially important word of advice to remember.... **Reciprocity is Yours to Expect!** Try pairing Communication with the Expectation of Reciprocation to jump-start or maintain that successful relationship. Also, please practice Relationship-Care to experience the Full Benefits of Relationship Reciprocity. How does that work? **Intentionally work on filling the Relationship Cup with your partner. It is critical that conversations around Relationship Reciprocity take place if you feel like it is lacking or if you feel like your relationship is just holding on.** Should you walk away from a Relationship that is lacking Reciprocity? The answer is it all depends. Remember at the beginning when I said, "Reciprocity is about Understanding"? **Well, start with getting yourself in a healthy space of Understanding who you are and what you need.** Explore how you can reach an optimal level of harmony within yourself to reach a harmonious level in your relationship. **If discord is the norm within yourself, lack of Relationship Reciprocation may be a contributing factor or the primary trigger.** If needed, seek professional help, and know that Reciprocation does not have to be an option for you in your relationship…**Reciprocation is the Relationship. It needs to be the Standard!**

**Be Well!**

**Good Vibes!**

- **Never stop giving. Do not allow the lack of reciprocity to stop you from being a powerful giver.**
- **Do you need reciprocity in your relationships? Is it necessary to the overall health of those coveted interactions?**
- **Define Reciprocity for yourself. Develop and idea of what that looks like and feels like for you.**

**Good Thoughts:**

# Cognitive Crisis: "Keep Your Mind Right"!

As we continue to try and adjust to the times we are living in, it is imperative that we consider the impact of all of this on our thinking processes. **Our Cognitive Health is rarely discussed in the times of this Covid-19 pandemic.** So, what does Cognitive really mean? *Cognitive health refers to our thinking skills, our thoughts, and the ability of the brain to reason.* We often speak about our feelings (Emotional Health) when discussing the current times. People may Feel Anxious, Depressed, Lonely, or Afraid. This blog post is focused on how people are thinking and processing this new normal as people are calling it. Although, there is a connection between our Emotional and Cognitive processes, I wanted to focus on the ladder to **help people understand the importance of keeping their mind right in this state of uncertain times.**

All this social distancing and quarantining has left many people alone with their thoughts. **Yes, we are always with our thoughts but so often life's distractions such as work, family, environmental shifts, and socializing in general create a much-needed escape from paying attention to what is going on in our heads.** Now, many of us are left to confront negative thoughts, distortions of the mind, and due to a clear lack of understanding of what is on the horizon…we must create hope from within. If you think about it, there is no clear consensus on how we will come out of this by those in positions of leadership. It is up to us to restructure our thoughts and visualize a favorable outcome for us, post this Covid-19 craziness. Even if it begins in our heads. **I know what you are thinking (pun intended), our thoughts do not always become reality but in this case, our thoughts don't need to come to life in order for them to help us be okay.** If our Cognitive System is healthy and utilized correctly, our thoughts can be a *place of peace and comfort.* How else will we cope with the loss of loved ones, seeing our hospitals packed with people just trying to survive, and not to mention our front-line workers who are risking their own lives just to make sure we're okay? It can literally break us down if we let it. **Let us shift our Thinking to make sure this does not happen!**

**Why is it a Cognitive Crisis? *(Corona Cognitive Crisis)* The word crisis is synonymous with danger and**

**troubling times.** Based on what I am seeing, I would say this is an accurate description. Agree? Think about it! (Big Pun again) Shout out to the rapper from the Bronx. Rest in peace. Okay, back on track...**We are on lock down!** Our kids are not attending school, movie theaters are closed, and socializing as we knew it is a thing of the past. **I literally must make sure that I am standing 6 ft. away from someone in the supermarket. Anybody else run out of the house and forget their mask? What about getting to your destination and realizing, "I forgot the $%@&*@%^ gloves"!!!** There is literally so much to think about nowadays. Our Cognitive Systems are working overtime. We must keep our system in a healthy state. ***An overworked Cognitive System can lead to Thinking processing issues, Anxiety, Depression, Anger, and more.*** See that?! There is the link between our cognitive processes and our Mental health. Poor cognitive functioning can lead to Mental health disorders, which can have an enormous impact on our immune systems. **Do not forget that there is the link between our cognitive health and our physical health as well.** It is time for us to put a greater emphasis on our Thinking Health and the amazing power it can have on helping us get through this in one piece.

**I love seeing the creation of home gyms, home workout plans, and even virtual gyms where people can exercise with each other online.** Our physical health is the most discussed system in today's times. Stay in shape, keep your weight down, you will look great, and feel great...yeah yeah yeah. All of these statements are true but if you have ever come in contact with someone in tip top physical condition that struggled with challenges in logic, rationality, or thinking processing than you know how important your Cognitive Health must be to truly function at your optimal level. **So, Dr. S...how do we get in our Cognitive Health bag? How do we get our Minds Right?** You already are by reading this blog post. One of the easiest ways to exercise our Cognitive system is to put our most important muscle (our brain) to work. **Taking in information that stimulates our thinking, triggers perspective taking, and even causes Cognitive Dissonance can be healthy.** Cognitive Dissonance is just a fancy way of saying a Conflict in our Thoughts. The difference with dissonance is that it often causes us distress. In this case, I am focusing on how **contrasting thoughts can lead us into a space of not only Thinking about our problems but Thinking about Solutions as well.** As we can see by all the dope creativity going on during these times, ***Crisis often leads to Creativity.*** That is a result of Healthy Cognitive Systems at work but there is more.

Starting your mornings with ***Meditation*** can be a great way of Calming and Centering our thoughts to start the day. Allow me to plug (shamelessly) my bestselling book, Good

Mornings: Wake-Up Calls for Life. Available Now and packed with positive morning messages for your Morning meditation exercises.

Okay, shameless plug complete. Let us get back to it. ***Gratitude Journals*** are another great Cognitive Exercise because it places our thoughts in a space of being grateful for what we have not what we lack. In the middle of a **pandemic storm, we can find peace in focusing our thoughts on all we do have to be thankful for right now.** Another great Cognitive tool, which happens to be my personal favorite is Music, specifically ***Hip-Hop***. Think of all the Thought-Provoking fires ignited by the beats, lyrics, and sounds of Hip-Hop. Music is literally a never-ending Cognitive Wellness Center. ***The artists are like Cognitive Trainers who allow us to utilize their sonic art as Cognitive Treadmills, which allow us to get our Thoughts Running.*** Do not forget about

***Visualization***. This is also a personal favorite of mine. Why do you think Vision Board Workshops have become the wave of every person who wants to create the life they have always dreamed of…Visualizing is a Thinking Exercise? A Cognitive Collage of images we desire, wish for, and hope for to make us happy. Visualizing allows us to Think of positive images, places, smells, and anything our six senses can imagine. It truly is a powerful way to relax us during these troubling times. **As I mentioned previously, I am of course all for manifesting and bringing all we visualize to life, but these Cognitive Exercises are about bring us a sense of calm.**

**Take care of your Cognitive Health during these times!** More than ever before, we must not allow Cognitive Captivity to take place. We cannot allow physical distancing to move us into a space in which we become trapped in by our own thoughts. We have the power to think beyond what is in front of us. **Just be Mindful that Cognitive Power is also rooted in the power to Choose.** You may hear some refer to our Thinking Power as being both a Gift and a Curse…but thankfully, **We get to Decide**! This post is about Choosing Our Cognitive Power to help us get through this unexplainable world-wind 2020 has seemingly placed us in. **Think Positive, Be Positive!** Our thoughts have a way of seeing us through the storms of life because we can Imagine the Sun.

**That means even amid this Covid-19 pandemic, Happiness exist. Just create it in your Mind, Right?!**

**Good Vibes!**

- **A healthy mind is the gateway for Happiness. Start with your thoughts to allow Happiness to flow.**
- **Get rid of Stinking Thinking. Eliminate thoughts of peril and replace with thoughts of positivity.**
- **Prepare yourself everyday with 3 positive thoughts. Affirm these thoughts by verbalizing them with confidence.**

**Below is my, "Cognitive-20". 20 Cognitive Exercises to help you in 2020. Be Well!**

1. Mediation
2. Gratitude Journals
3. Music
4. Visualization
5. Reading
6. Writing
7. Perspective Taking
8. Debating
9. Problem Solving
10. Cognitive Games
11. Chess
12. Word Searches

13. Scrabble
14. Trivia
15. Video Games
16. Psychological Thrillers
17. Learn a Language or New Hobby
18. Talking to a friend who Challenges You
19. Become a Lifetime Learner
20. Research a Societal Issue

**Good Thoughts:**

# Triggered Again...but I am Still Healing!

Anyone else over all this Covid-19, Global Pandemic, Social Distance, and Grab your mask/gloves craziness? It still does not seem real sometimes as you travel out and see nothing but covered faces and empty streets. Is this how you imagined your 2020 would turn out to be? I am certain that no one had this mapped out on their vision boards for this year. **It is like we come up for air and then suddenly we are dragged back underwater and fighting to survive once again.** This constant battle or ongoing struggle to survive is exactly what those who have experienced Trauma must push through daily. **I do not believe we will fully comprehend the impact of this ordeal on our Mental and Emotional health for months to follow but believe me, many people have been re-triggered by these events.** This is a lesson about Healing that we all must learn. There is no ending date. Yes, we can heal and resolve negative feelings around past trauma but to say that the healing is done, is inaccurate. **Healing is a continuous process of growing, learning, discovering, setbacks, and comebacks!**

I know…I know, you were doing so well. You worked through those past traumas, stopped beating yourself up about the pain, realized that the things you experienced no longer had to control you, and then…. A Global Pandemic!? Great, now I must be socially distant (which, on the low I secretly enjoy) even though I know it is not completely healthy for my Anxiety. **Not to mention my health, overeating, pressure to be active, and the obvious uncertainty of what the future of life will look like is really overwhelming.** While everyone is discussing the impact of the virus on our Physical Health, watching a tally of those who have died from Covid-19, is a daily trigger for many. As a Mental-Health Therapist, it pains me that "news" networks would continue to avoid the simple act of posting, "Those Who Have Recovered" on their little numbers tally every day. **It lets me know that we are still so far behind in the understanding of Mental-Health Wellness and the power of Positive Thinking as well as Positive Optics.** I honestly believe this to be true…the more Positive Things, Words, Statements, and Images we see; the better we will feel. Of course, keeping people informed is important but is there another agenda? **Is there something to**

**be gained by pushing Fear over Hope?** Some may argue that both processes are rooted in unreal expectations, but I would argue that **a person imagining Life, Healing, and Peace will fare much better than someone seeing images of Death, Despair, and Chaos.**

Triggered? Yes! Healing? Yes! **There is nothing wrong with admitting that this pandemic stuff has opened old wounds for you.** I am sure it seemed like the old scars were fading and the volume on the memories had been turned down to the point that you could no longer hear the pain. I am not going to even suggest that you just pick yourself up and simply dust yourself off and get back to it. I am not trying to minimize what anyone may be feeling right now. **I do think it is critical that people allow themselves to feel all the range of emotions their experiencing currently. Allow yourself to be vulnerable and honest.** If it hurts, say it hurts. If you are afraid, say you are scared. The reason why this is so important is that our emotions should not be synonymous with bars that hold us captive. **This can be mentally draining as we turn all our feelings inward, literally scarring our insides and feeding the powers of Trauma and Anxiety, all over again.** Where can you find your emotional freedom? I believe the answer to that question lies in your power to **embrace this idea of a continuous flow of Healing that occurs even during uncertain times.**

**Nothing is Healthier than Healing.** Think about it. In life we are certain to be faced with battles, storms, and difficult times. Our ability to Heal and Grow from those moments is what makes Life liberating. **Although, we should not praise the setback of being re-triggered, we can be secure in the restoring power of Healing Again.** The reason being is that You Never Stopped Healing! When you adopt a mentality of ongoing mental nurturing and emotional wellness, you build up protective energies against Mental Viruses. **Mental viruses invade your thinking, feeling, and behavioral systems.** You can quickly find yourself returning to the same dark places you worked so hard to come out from. Remember this, Your Healing occurs because You Are the Light during dark times. **It is a process of discovery where you begin to realize your power to illuminate from within. Trauma no longer has a place to hide.** It is like glowing from the inside out and feeling brand new. Here is the key. **If you are the light, being triggered only activates your healing powers. It does not damage you.** Fear does not control you. Anxiety does not have to become you. Go ahead Heal. Remember how much you have already overcome. **Keep glowing and stay positive. Being triggered does not have to incapacitate you or stop you from moving forward. Keep Healing!**

**Good Vibe Tips:**

**1)** Declare, "I am Thriving not Surviving".

**2)** Breathe and Release your feelings.

**3)** Gratitude Grounds Us, Practice Gratitude Daily.

**4)** Journal Your Thoughts.

**5)** Allow Positive Energies into Your Space.

**Good Thoughts:**

# "Thank you for the opportunity but I quit"! A 4-week lesson about Purpose.

It was a great day. I received notice that Rutgers University was interested in hiring me for a great position as a consultant/trainer. This would be a great way to transition from direct practice and focus on doing some more work to impact the systems that provide services to so many of the youth I have worked with for years. It has been quite a while since I had a job and although I was excited, I was somewhat worried about the transition from entrepreneur to employee. There is nothing wrong with being an employee but if you have been working for yourself for the last 5 years, the move could be a little difficult. Anyway, it was too late to turn back now. (So, I thought).

First, there was the tour of the unit and my cozy little cubicle that I would be spending most of my time. "Never had a cubicle", I thought to myself, but I will make it work. What is the big deal? I already started to feel a little uneasy about the idea of containing all my creative energy into a small little section of space. The environment was super quiet. No noisy students, no morning announcements, and no impromptu visits from kids. Once again, not a big deal because it has been several years since I left my school district post, so the idea of a peaceful place was somewhat enjoyable (So I thought).

As weeks went by, I had some genuinely nice interactions with my colleagues. All of them nice people and extremely supportive during my transition but I just felt out-of-place, right away. I sat through two very intense orientations about rules, dress codes, working during snowstorms, and buying into the Rutgers way. At this point, the uneasiness started to build, and I found myself saying on the drive home, "What did I get myself into"? I started revisiting the reason why I was transitioning from my remarkably successful practice that had grown over the last 5 years. I was developing new ideas, establishing new professional relationships, but still felt like I needed a change. Maybe, in hindsight I just needed a break but how could I leave. I just accepted this position and received high praise for what I would add to the team so how could I let these people down? I decided that maybe these are just some growing pains and I needed to be patient.

I would soon realize that there was no amount of patience that would change how I was feeling. I knew what the problem was, but I was ignoring the signs. I was experiencing some challenges in self-care. I was also growing frustrated with the slow process in which my new endeavor, Mental-Hop (Mental-Health Education & Hip-Hop Culture) was taking off. I seemed to forget that my previous endeavor, Project EmpowerMENt required three plus years of hard-work, sleepless nights, and hustle before I even had an opportunity to pilot a program. Why was I giving up so quickly with Mental-Hop? I got comfortable and honestly…lazy about my purpose. I convinced myself that maybe my purpose was somewhere else. The prestigious Rutgers University Campus would be the place where I would find my purpose and cruise into the sunset of a 25 year-long career with a nice pension, great benefits, and the RU logo on my resume. Well, that dream ended quickly when I was so frustrated about the idea of going into work the next day, I already decided the fate of my relationship with Rutgers. After only 4 long weeks of service, I met with my supervisor (have not had one of those in a while either) and gave her the news. Of course, the typical response of disappointment, some slight annoyance with my decision to resign, and some discussion about whether we could work it out. The answer was "no". I only needed 4 weeks to see that my dreams and purpose mattered more.

I gave the customary 2-weeks' notice, although if I were asked to leave that day, I would not have argued. I want to make this clear! There was absolutely nothing wrong with

Rutgers University. There was everything wrong with ME at Rutgers University. See, I am not your conventional Therapist/Doctor/Creative. I enjoy the noise of a busy school. I hate the idea of a cubicle or an extremely quite workplace where everyone whispers to each other. This move allowed me some time to reflect on the why behind my attempted move to a larger organizational structure. It was in that reflection that I realized that I needed to be more appreciative of the work I was doing and take some time to enjoy the fruits of my labor. I needed to get back to work on my passion and purpose in a more strategic way. I needed to STOP BEING LAZY! I fell off when it came to the work ethic of my latest project, Mental-Hop. I immediately started planning new strategies and approaches to accomplish some Mental-Hop goals. In no time, I started seeing actual results from a renewed energy I had in this purpose-driven work. I also started to be more thankful for the journey I had already traveled. Sometimes, we get complacent and forget how far we have come on the road to accomplishing our goals. I vowed to never allow myself to be in that place again.

I must thank Rutgers University so much for both the opportunity of something new and for helping me to walk away from that new thing, I never needed. Sometimes you need to polish off that diamond you already have before you run out and purchase the diamond you think is so much better.

It only took me 4 weeks to realize this powerful lesson. How long will you stay at your "Rutgers University"? How long will you neglect your diamond that only needs a little polishing to be brand new again? Find your passion again and recharge your Purpose. Do not run from your Purpose because it did not manifest in your timeframe. Maybe you are about to walk away, just as the manifestation is set to begin. If you plant the seeds, water them daily, and nurture them daily…. you do not have to look for a new garden. You need to believe in the process enough to stay, wait, and see!

**Just know when it is time to start but more importantly when it is time leave!**

**Good Vibes!**

- **Sometimes we step out of our purpose, just to feel connected to something else. It is okay to realize that it was not for you and step away if you need to.**
- **Do not worry about what other may think of you. It is important that you own your decisions and learn from them in the process.**
- **You are the diamond. Keep shining and polishing your skills to stay valuable.**

**Good Thoughts:**

# The Dreamer's Dilemma?

At the crossroads and facing another sleepless night, a dreamer works without rest on their passion. It is a beautiful new project that has kept the dreamer eagerly writing new plans and strategizing ways to execute with success. It is almost like they can visualize the wave of support that will come from family and friends. They can hear it now, "this is awesome", "I'm definitely behind you, just tell me where to get it", "wow, you did it…I'm so proud of you". It is enough love to lead a dreamer right into a state of euphoria as that small, tiny, and minute thought has grown into a successful social venture that will change the world. It is utterly amazing except for one thing…the dreamer has become a victim of their own incredible power. They are DREAMING! Now faced with the dreaded "Dreamer's Dilemma". A diagnosis that often plaques dreamers with overwhelming stress, countless hours of uncertainty, and many moments of frustration, but the greatest symptom of the "Dreamer's

Dilemma" is that agonizing question, "should I even continue"?

The reality of the dreamer is often much different than the reality they have created in their mind, post launch of their world changing dream. Many have given words of encouragement, support, and those somewhat cynical emojis people love but I cringe at 🙌✊💪💯 which often replace actually BUYING products or services that the Dreamer has launched, relaunched, and re-relaunched.

It is enough to cause a major dilemma. Maybe I should just scrap this dream and make the dreamers death 💀 decision…" kill the dream". It is incredibly frustrating, heartbreaking, and I do not know…annoying? To think that your brilliant idea did not take off like Facebook, Uber, or even the Pet Rock. I mean people even ran out and got that spinning thing for kids, surely, they would support my idea. Right? Nope, your idea is not the cool spinning thing. It is being supported more like the Shark Tank's dumbest ideas. During all the thoughts of giving up, the Dreamer has embedded in the psyche a "Dreamer's Dilemma" defense mechanism. It is also their incredible power to dream. The dreamer cannot turn it off! As one dream fades, another one suddenly pops up. Not necessarily a new dream but a new dream to enhance the previous dream. Yes, it is truly crazy to those who are not dreamers but once again it is those crazy dreamers that have changed the world. So, here is the bottom line. A dreamer is always in a dilemma, but it is a beautiful dilemma because it is an extremely uncomfortable place. Yes, discomfort is the designed destiny of the dreamer. It is the creative space in which the dreamer grows. Not sure if it is going to work is uncomfortable. Not selling items is uncomfortable. Looking those people that claim to support you but never actually do in the eye and smile is extremely uncomfortable but then there's growth!

Dreamers are the farmers and caretakers to the seeds that change the world. One may say it like this, Dreamers Change the World. So, I pose this question to you. What is the "Dreamer's Dilemma"? The answer may be summed up like this, the "Dreamer's Dilemma" is to Dream or to Keep Dreaming. Dreams never die because there will always be a new dream for the dreamer. A new seed that requires the dreamer's water and feeding. Keep dreaming dreamers. We need you…the world needs you!

-Dr. S aka Just a Dreamer!

**Good Vibes!**

- **It is your responsibility to keep your dreams alive. So, what will you do with your dreams?**

- **The world needs Dreamers. Our innovation, creativity, and progress will be sparked by the imagination of the Dreamers.**
- **Keep watering and nurturing your Dreams like you are expecting a plentiful harvest of greatness to grow.**

**Good Thoughts:**

# Stop waiting for approval!

Moving through life while carrying dreams and goals is challenging enough. Why complicate things more by seeking approval from others to take that leap of faith towards your goals? Validation from others when it comes to chasing your dreams can be a dream killer. There seems to be this notion that before we make a major move or leap, we need to seek out permission from everyone in our circle before moving forward. Although it is cool to have everyone on board before taking off, this flight needs to soar regardless because of what is at stake if you stay figuratively grounded.

Being empowered means that you are more than equipped to jump without being pushed by others. You are more than capable of riding without passengers beside you. You are more than willing to go at it alone than wait for others to decide whether your vision fits their lens. This is about you! This is not about being selfish or unconcerned about the feelings of others. This is about prioritizing your dreams over the opinions, uncertainties, doubt, or insecurities of others. This is about living without regrets and being able to look back with confidence and happiness because you never waited. You realized that approval is needed for those not in a boss position but that is where you are. You are the boss of your dreams, the owner of your ambition, and sole traveler of your purpose.

So, go! Go with confidence and believe in yourself. Do not let anything stop you or deter you from moving forward with those dreams and goals that keep you up at night. Sometimes to grow, we must go alone. Free of permission, approval, or validation from others. We must be brave enough to face failure and strong enough to seek success. Let your ambition inspire others to do the same, as you speak this into existence, **"I'm no longer going to wait, I'm no longer going to ask…. Your approval is not required. It's time for me to fly".** You have the power to activate energies through the words that pour from your mouth. Of course, it would be great to have the support of others but understand that good things do not always come to those who wait…sometimes we must be the catalyst. Go ahead and make it happen!

**Good Vibes!**

- **Have you ever waited on someone to else approve something you already had the power to do on your own?**
- **Do you have a Boss mindset? That means that you are owning your choices and not waiting for others to cosign for you.**
- **You are not required to get permission for your happiness. It is all yours!**

**Imagination…your secret weapon against being stuck!**

**It is easy to get caught in the mental matrix of stagnation or uncertainty about which direction to go at times.** At any point along this journey you may find yourself slowly drifting off track. You may even hit a point where absolutely no movement is taking place. Not because you do not want to or because the desire is not there. It is more a function of getting stuck in the routine of dream chasing or just living life for that matter. The "stuck" energy is a function of society that pushes us to just go, go, go, and that approach gives us little time to reflect and enjoy the process. That is when imagination can be used as a secret weapon to destroy those "stuck" or trapped feelings.

*"The world of reality has its limits; the world of imagination is boundless".*

**-Jean-Jacques Rousseau**

Our imagination allows us to mentally escape the monotonous and redundant times that may come on at various times throughout our journey. I truly believe we need to build in imagination breaks, not in a super formal way where you place "imagination break" on your schedule, right after "boring meeting with higher-ups" but more of a moment of peace, which triggers imaginative thoughts. **Keep in mind that imagination is so powerful and cool that it can happen almost anywhere.** Have you ever been in the loudest and busiest place, only to find yourself zoning out? Maybe at the height of the most seemingly stressful times, you picture yourself on a warm and sandy beach with just the sounds of the water quieting your thoughts. I see imagination as a critical tool in self-care. It is closely tied to the tool of positive self-imagery, which therapists like me use to help clients with anxiety or even anger.

**The process of using our imagination is often pushed as a child but somewhere along the way, people stop using it.** It is almost as if life slowly kills off our imagination so that we can fall in line with the factory, assembly line, and rat race mentality which stifles happiness and freedom. I not only want you to never lose your imagination, I want you to use it more than ever before. I want you to imagine yourself at that beautiful beach location or riding down the street in that car you have always wanted. I want you to imagine yourself in the house of your dreams or traveling to another country to feed people in need. Our imagination is not only the secret weapon against feeling stuck, it is also the fuel to our dreams and ambitions. It is the quintessential companion to hope and the necessary running-mate to faith. Our ability to use our imagination in a very conscious way can unlock new levels of creativity and success. Listen, being stuck is terrible but staying stuck is like a slow death. Obviously, being stuck or in a place where we are not moving is not death in the physical but be careful.

**If we allow ourselves to stay in a place of being "stuck", our dreams, ambitions, and goals will slowly**

**fade away.** That fading away from a mental, emotional, and introspective standpoint can trigger increased levels of sadness and even depression. Remember the connection between our physical health and emotional health is real. Increased levels of "stuck", may lead to increased anxiety or even hyper-tension, which is never good for our over-all physical health. Imagination gives us hope. That hope moves us to keep pushing and keeps a necessary fire burning inside of us. Imagination fuels our motivation and movement, which defies stagnation or being stuck.

So, here is your homework. Keep teaching kids to use their imagination but most importantly, live life where you never lose your imagination. **Keep yourself armed with a weapon that no one can take away.** Your IMAGINATION is yours to keep but only if you continue to use it and allow it to activate all the positive energies within you.

Imagine what great and beautiful thing you will do next? go ahead and imagine!

**Good Vibes!**

- **Never stop imagining. See beyond the circumstances in front of you and create something of wonder.**
- **The mind is powerful, whatever you visualize inside of your mind, can become a reality.**

- **Imagination is vast and without limits. There are no walls to your imagination.**

**Good Thoughts:**

# Hip-Hop and Mental Health: The bridge nobody wants to build....so it seems?!

**There is no denying the power of hip-hop culture and its ability to impact generations of listeners, artist, producers, break dancers, graffiti artist, and DJs around the world.** Hip-hop represents an energy that is driven by the people for the people. Whenever a force of this magnitude continues to top every other genre by leaps and bounds, we should be utilizing its power to transform systems. I honestly believe that hip-hop can change the world in a positive way. Like any form of power, when put into the wrong hands it can have the opposite effect and negatively influence a multitude of people as well as the world. Now I know it seems that I am making hip-hop out to be the savior of the people and that's not my intention, although hip-hop to a degree has saved my life in many aspects by giving me a forum to express my feelings in a positive way. What I am simply implying is that hip-hop can be a tool of change within the education system, community, issues impacting youth, and in the system at the forefront of this post...Mental Health.

Let us be clear, until recently discussions about mental health in hip-hop have been taboo. This is typically due to the stigma around mental health and the notion that discussions about feelings and emotions within hip-hop culture were frowned upon and looked at as soft or weak. Even though the hardest rhyme marksmen from **Biggie, Jay-Z, Nas, Ice-Cube, Lox, and NWA used hip-hop to express feelings with eloquence and introspection it is still often looked at in a negative way. Even more current artist such as J-Cole, Wale, Dave East, and Meek** use hip-hop to paint an audio picture of feelings that resonate within them as they release fury within the studio booth. We are not talking about selling a few CDs or having a couple of thousand downloads. The artist mentioned above have millions and millions of listeners worldwide. People who sometimes blindly download their music based on their names and previous work. That is a powerful weapon in any hands but whether it is used for good or evil depends on many factors. I believe the artist have the power to shift the discussion of mental health from one that is stigmatized to one that is empowering and world-changing for the next generation.

So how do we begin to develop this bridge? We start with authentic, non-judgmental, and very practical discussions about mental health. Most importantly these discussions should come from the artist themselves in forums where young people get to see, connect, and speak directly with them. It would require a level of vulnerability that artist clearly can actualize just as they do in their music. I am not talking about a performance. **I am talking about a town-hall forum, where artist tell their stories of loss, anxiety, sadness, happiness, loneliness, depression, and mindfulness**. It is within that dialog and exchange that the bridge is created and a stigma the size of a mountain is cracked, eventually crumbled using hip-hop as the primary machine. Once we understand that hip-hop is a culture and so much more than just a genre of music, we will begin to use it to impact other issues of concern such as poverty, homelessness, chronic community violence, domestic abuse, and social injustice. The bridge between hip-hop and mental health must be developed through collaborative efforts between the music, arts, education, community, government, and mental health stakeholders. The collaboration must also be void of ego, greed, and ill intentions. I say this because it would be naive for me to believe that everyone wants to see our youth awake, conscious, and mindful as it pertains to the messages within the music they consume or lyrics from artist. In fact, some people would never read this post because it contradicts all intentions of keeping our young people sleep, in despair, and burdened with increased anger, sadness, and worry.

*"The thing about hip-hop today is it's smart, it's insightful. The way they can communicate a complex message in a very short space is remarkable".*

**-Barack Obama**

That is fine because this post is not for those people. **This post is for those individuals that grew up on a culture of hip-hop that was life changing and mind-blowing**. Maybe it is for the person who wants to help a young man feel more comfortable about expressing his feelings. Maybe it is for the woman who is focused on empowering our little girls to break through the male configured and socially constructed glass ceilings, at any level. How about the student who is being bullied because they speak different or do not have the latest Jordans to fit in with the crowd in the school cafeteria? Maybe it is just that teacher who is trying to find a creative way to help her students learn math or reading. The writing is on the wall. Hip-Hop is here to stay and although many will argue that it will never be the same, it is power will remain because hip-hop has withstood the test of time unlike many other genres that have slowly faded away. Hip-hop and mental health may seem far apart but there is a bridge being built. **Just like any bridge that is currently in development, it takes time and an enormous amount of patience.** So what?! The process is beautiful, so let us enjoy watching the construction of a powerfully connective structure that is the bridge between Hip-Hop and Mental Health!

**Now put on some Biggie, The sky is the Limit and be positively patient as Hip-Hop once again changes the world!**

Good Vibes!

- **Did you ever consider the connection between Hip-Hop and Mental-health?**
- **There is healing power in music. Put on some music medicine and take the pain away.**
- **Have your favorite albums and artists on standby when you need a Mental boost.**

**Good Thoughts:**

# If you are being stretched, pulled, and pressed...just stay right there! (Growing Pains).

**You may be in a season of growing and feel yourself being pushed out of your comfort zone.** It is the type of feeling that has you questioning, "why me" and the answer is clear, you are being prepped for something greater. A child often never feels the physical changes that take place during their stages of growth. They usually hear about it from others or as they pass by mirrors, notice gradual changes in appearance or their height. When we are older, we assume that our physical growth spurt has ended, and we proceed to accept that this is the way we will be. That may be entirely true from a physical aspect but what about our mental and emotional growth? What about our growth as an individual, as it relates to life and evolving as a person? These changes may not be as noticeable as a physical change, but change is always happening. Remember it is the only thing that is constant…you are changing as you read this blog post.

The title is meant to push you to a place of introspection and reflection regarding areas of your life where elevated levels of discomfort are taking place. **It may feel like relationships are being strained or finances are being pulled to a point where it seems like too much to handle.** There may be a strong desire to retreat and go back to that place of comfort, that place where everything is familiar to you…often a place where things just seem easier. I urge you, do not allow yourself to go back there or even travel to that place physically or mentally. The stretching and pulling that is being experienced is healthy for you. In fact, it is critical to your growth, success, and progress. The similarities between the processes of growth and change have been discussed for years because both operate simultaneously. There will never be an instance where you will have one without the other. The awesome thing about the way this tandem works is that in the end, you benefit from their incredible ability to pull and push on you until you are ready. I know, until "I'm ready for what"? That really depends on you and the journey you are on as it relates to what you desire in life.

*"Everyone wants to live on top of the mountain, but all the happiness and growth occurs while you're climbing it."*

**-Andy Rooney**

I sum it up like this. On the other side of the pulling, pressing, and stretching is the good stuff. The good stuff is all those things you desired but were not prepared for. Maybe it is that new relationship. Maybe it is that new business opportunity. Maybe it is getting into that college. **Anything that you desire will require a new and improved version of yourself. The creation of a new you is what is taking place during the pulling, pressing, and stretching.** You are literally being challenged to see if you can handle what is about to come. Your patience is being pulled. Your determination will be pressed, and your faith will be stretched. You are growing and evolving into a newer and more improved version of yourself. It is not only great for you, but it becomes a story of resilience that can be shared with others. Not everyone will be in this season at the same time so do not expect others to always sympathize with you as your growing pains are taking place.

**Just know that you are being prepared for the next level through these changes and the good stuff is waiting for you on the other side.**

**Good Vibes!**

- **Growing hurts but it is that good pain that puts you in a better position in the end.**
- **Think of some moments in your life in which you were in pain but in the end, felt better.**
- **You do remember how they make diamonds. If you are going through that same process, imagine how you will be shining in the end.**

**Good Thoughts:**

# The perfect Love story.... starring you!

**So many people are intrigued by the perfect love story.** That movie where the conflicts, obstacles, and challenges always lead to that ending in which love is found and happiness wins. Thank goodness for entertainment because so often life does not imitate art and we are left with an idea of love that so often only exist in major Hollywood pictures. There is hope though when it comes to love and landing that winning audition in the next epic love story.

Here is the good news, there is no casting couch or lines of actors/actresses waiting to show off their talents for the leading role. Do not worry about memorizing a long script filled with romantic scenes or tear-jerking moments that just make you melt. Although none of the above steps are necessary for this narrative, which will surely change your life, it will require some moves on your part. Are you ready?

**First, approach the nearest mirror within your proximity and prepare your voice for your love story debut.** Here it goes, you need to say it like you mean it, "I love myself. I know I am not perfect, but I am worthy of love. I accepted myself 100% and understand that I am a work of art that continues to evolve. I am in great expectation of where I am headed on my journey and will love myself without condition". Congratulations, you have just accepted the role of the leading woman or man in a story that will last forever…if you let it.

**See, love is so powerful that it initiates within you first and foremost**. Once you truly embrace who you are and value yourself, new levels of understanding occur, and love becomes so much easier. To reciprocate love, we must understand how to pour love into ourselves without condition. So often, love fails because people want to act in the realm of the "Love Idea". That is the concept, bells, and whistles of love, which breaks hearts and ruins relationships. Let us be clear, love is not perfect but when it is authentic, it is intentionally perfect. This simply means that love which comes from the right place, should never be accused of being wrong. Love that starts from your own heart and resonates within you is imperfectly perfect and exactly what love stories are made of.

**So, here is the question, have you auditioned for the starring role in your perfect love story?** Or are you waiting for someone else to step in for that role? Remember that love for self is not vain, selfish, or self-defeating. It is beautiful, authentic, and necessary. So, lights, camera, and action…the perfect love story is about to begin. No matter what the critics say, the award will always go to you in the most incredible, sensational, and magical love story ever.

**The perfect love story…starring you!**
**Good Vibes!**

- **Self-Love is not selfish love. It is an intense acceptance of who you are and embracing imperfect perfection of your existence.**
- **How can you start showing yourself some love today?**
- **The spotlight is all yours. I love myself because, I am…………**

**Good Thoughts:**

# Do not hate the Storms, while waiting on the Sun!

It is really all about perception, right?** Life has taught me so many lessons, but this may be the most important of them all. Our perception is a powerful and valuable tool, if used correctly. Perception gives us the ability to see beyond what our physical eyes can see and feel deeper that than the reality we are experiencing. I have come to understand perception as the power to look at a situation, circumstance, or experience with a full lens instead of a skewed view based on past knowledge, people's opinions, or ideas.

Gary Zukav makes a great observation about perception when stating, ***"What is behind your eyes holds more power than what is in front of them"***. So, perception is about a deeper exploration of what is being presented and I believe to gain some greater understanding, which should benefit us as well as others. So, what does this have to do with storms or the sun? Well, no this is not some scientific, super metaphoric, or confusing post about weather or energy. This is a very practical way of seeing the world and the good times as well as bad times that impact us all at some point in life. This is about how we can create value even during difficult times.

The storms (tough times) are real, there is no denying the presence of life storms that seem to come in groups of 100 and at the exact time in which we feel that the sun will never go away. **Let us face it, storms suck!** We often feel alone during them, life just seems colder during their presence, and it just seems like we will be stuck in their presence forever. That is the reality of a crisis in our relationship, medical issues that impact our lives or our loved one's life, or the common storm of more bills than money. This is when the power of perception should be a hammer in the "How do I deal with this" toolbox. We should all have one of these toolboxes handy. Remember, perception is about seeing beyond the reality or storm you are facing. Let us try to practice the power of perception by searching for a deeper understanding of some of life's storms.

- Storms often startle us: Perception= "Maybe I was headed in the wrong direction and needed to be reminded to stop and think about it".

- Storms can leave us feeling lonely: Perception= "Maybe I needed some time alone to evaluate where I am and learn to believe in myself".
- Storms can destroy things: Perception= "Maybe this relationship is bad for me and it needed to be interrupted, disrupted, and destroyed so I can have something better".
- Storms can lead to starting over: Perception= "Maybe I made some wrong choices that led me to this point, this can be a new opportunity to get back on track".

**It seems through the power of perception that the storms themselves are not the problem**, it is the pulling, stretching, and pressing while we are in the storm that moves us to hate the storms of life. So, then we begin we start to use perception and realize that storms are not only opportunities for us to prepare for the sun that will soon come, storms are vital and necessary for our growth in life. The flower will not grow without the rain of a powerful storm. Just like that same flower depends on the sun for its nourishment to blossom. It is when we begin to shift our perception that we realize, hating the storm is the worst thing for us to do. We would be better off embracing the storms of life. I know what you are thinking, "another crazy psycho doctor with a crazy theory that we should love the bad times that happen in life", actually no but this Dr. Crazy does have a practical idea.

As you move forward and from this day on, do not hate the storm. Just be more aware that while you are in the storm, you are growing, being prepared, and definitely changing. You are becoming ready for the sunshine, which will inevitably arrive at the exact time is needs to in your life. Trying using perception in other situations as well. A job loss may mean, your season at that place is up and something new is awaiting. The distance in a relationship may be communicating that you both need time to appreciate each other more and when you return your love for each other will be stronger. If you gained nothing more from this post, try using perception a little bit more. Try increasing your level of awareness when tough times (storms) show up. Lastly, try creating a "How do I deal with this" toolbox, everyone should have one of those.

**The storms will come but let us not hate them. After all, the sun will come out tomorrow!**

**Good Vibes!**

- **What do the storms of life teach us about the sun?**
- **Think of some storms you have encountered that rocked your boat. Now, list the ways you made it through to experience the sun.**
- **Do you ever talk to your storm? Declare to your storm that this is not the end.**

**Good Thoughts:**

# No More Discounts...You deserve the best!

**There is no time like the present to take inventory of how you have been treated by others.** Remember that you have control of how others treat you. You can be either accepting or challenging regarding the behaviors of others towards you. This is sometimes easier said than done, especially if you are concerned about being perceived as unkind, have low self-esteem, or tend to shy away from confrontation. This is the moment of truth. After reading this life changing, introspective, and self-reflective article; you will need to reconsider how you view yourself as well as others.

**YOU DESERVE THE BEST!** This is a declaration of change and a conscious choice to take back your power as it pertains to expectation and value. I challenge you to walk into a Rolls Royce dealer and just browse the selection of hand-crafted vehicles in the showroom. I want you to notice the detail, pay attention to the craftsmanship, and the quality will be evident as soon as you walk in. This is exactly how you should view yourself when it comes to your interactions with others but let us return to the dealer for the primary point. As you approach the dealer and he indicate the vehicle you have suddenly fell in love with has a price tag of $200,000, please do not faint or yell "TWO HUNDRED THOUSAND DOLLARS"!!! As you try to wrap your mind around this amount of money for a car, the value of this fine piece of metal has been decided and trust me, someone is going to but it.

Just imagine trying to get the salesman to come down on that price just a little. Let us say you are willing to pay $150,000 and as you make your offer, the salesman laughs and calmly tells you "this is a Rolls, there is no negotiating on the price". That exact statement is how you should see your worth as it pertains to how you are treated by others, the level of respect you receive from others, and your level of expectation from others. **You too must see yourself as a precious, handcrafted, and immaculately detailed work of art.** This mindset will put others on notice that you will demand only the best from them, and discounts will no longer be given. It does not mean you are unkind or afraid or over-confident. It simply means that you understand your worth and expect to be treated like you deserve. **You are that special. You are that** deserving and soon people will approach you like to Rolls Royce of a person you are.

Now go and be that dream car of a person.... all $200,000 plus of a person!

Good Vibes!

- Understand and appreciate your value. Do not accept less than full price for your greatness.
- How is your self-esteem? Are there past experiences that have impacted your self-esteem? Start to highlight your strengths. Make a big deal about your superpowers and share them with others.
- You are an immaculate work of art. Let you name be elegance when spoken by others.

**Good Thoughts:**

# Black Self-Care! "Black Love, Black Solidarity, and Black Community Compassion".

The blackest piece of coal sits and awaits its fate. The pressing and crumbling of its current state in the most stressful conditions imaginable, it evolves into something else. Although, now transformed into the most coveted stone known to man, this flawless diamond still embodies the elements of its original state. Everyone loves the diamond, but no one wants the coal. That is until we begin to talk about Black Diamonds. Black Diamonds are seen as a threat to the livelihood of other diamonds so to return them back to their original state, there is a process of reversal that must take place. You are now witnessing the, "Again" in the most coded, highly recognizable, and blood red hat back-dropped statement that is "Make America Great Again".

We are currently living in a critical time for Black People. The year is 2020 and change is on the horizon. We are at the most stressful part of our journey, the crossroads. The dissonance is critical as we stand facing two different paths to consider. Path A would be a return to the aforementioned, "Again" or also Path A, a journey to the return of something even more powerful than the "Again". I am talking about a Return to the time of Black Love, Black Solidarity, and Black Community Compassion. To Matter will not be enough...to simply exists will not be enough for our value is far greater. Therefore, we often feel we are being hunted. Just like the mighty elephant for its tusks or the magnificent rhino for its horn...what Black people possess is something of a threat to many and the only way to insure that Black Diamonds don't reach the market in masses is to intensify the systemic process of strategically reversing Black Diamonds back to Black Coal...because Black Coal has no purpose. It is worthless...so they mistakenly believe!

We are in for the fight of our lives and I am mentally and emotionally exhausted. I'm sorry but I do not have the energy to recap all of the murders by White Police Officers or the blatant examples of White Privilege in parks, stores, workplaces, educational institutions, court rooms, driving in your car, sitting in your house, or while jogging on a country road. Within all this blog talk around Black Diamonds, I promise you...this is a blog post about Black Self-Care! It really is! In my conversations with Black People, there seems to be a consensus emotion most commonly present...that is best described as, "I'm Tired"! Cups are empty, tanks are empty, and energy is low. How do we sustain this fight for our Black Diamond Lives? How do we find the strength to continue our Resistance? We have been literally dragged into the fire (Again!), the pressing, and crushing racist spaces to bring us back to an earlier state. Is this a Movement or a Moment? The answer lies within our ability to sustain.

Sustain...Our Lives depend on our ability to sustain Black Love. That is the Love for Our Brothers and Sisters on the frontlines, back-lines, and everywhere in between. This Love is not that fleeting love that ends when media and social media decides to pull the curtain down on what they hope will be our moment. This Black Love came from your ancestors...it is embedded in the very DNA that has provided you with the power to overcome conflict, resist division, decrease ego, and combat hating on one another. The primary weapons utilized to defeat Black Love are hate and division within our own circle. Your enemy never has to show up. They simply plant the seeds, design the conditions, and watch our demise from a far...All the while screaming, "Look how they treat each other...Look at that Black on Black crime". These are tactics of division, but Black Love will prevail if we stick to Love that is authentically articulated and empathetically displayed through our actions. Love your Black brother and Black sister with all you have within you...More Than Ever Before! Let it energize you as you energize each other. Let it rejuvenate you...Be Happy for Your Brothers and Sisters! Allow it to Heal You! Black Love is just one of the many medicines that allow Our Collective Healing to happen during this season...but what else? Stay Solid!

Let us find strength and support in Black Solidarity. Within the word solidarity, you will find the word solid. That Black Diamond is solid...never forget that! Solidarity refers to unity and agreement. It is great to have people from all walks of life, march with us as we demand to live but nothing will be more powerful than our very own Black Solidarity. If you really think and analyze it, Black solidarity is the key to Our Collective Black Empowerment. I keep hearing people say, "If we could just get on the same page"! "If we could just come together". "If we could only understand our power". All these statements are calls for Black Solidarity as a primary component to disrupting the systems and systematic stifling of our upward collective mobility. Black Solidarity is Black Self-Care because it provides support from others, inspiration from others, knowledge from others, and the much-needed push from others when we feel like we are breaking apart. Black Solidarity keeps us whole when we feel overwhelmed and burned out from a system that has thrown these Black Diamonds back into the fire to bring us back to a state of coal. If they only knew...that the coal is the power!

There is power within our Black Community! Right now, more than ever before, we must wrap our arms around our communities. We need to have a compassionate heart for our most vulnerable areas. Compassion is founded on patience, caring, empathy, and support. All of which is needed during this critical season of shifting that we are experiencing. Hug our Black Communities by patronizing Black Businesses, Mentoring Black Youth, Buying Property in Black Communities, Denouncing Acts of Violence and Abuse, and Advocating for Black Therapy spaces...these are just few examples of how Compassion can transform. There is something about compassion...it is intensely caring and giving.

When your cup is running low, I will help you fill yours up again. When you feel stressed and you just do not seem to care as much, I will remind you of how special you are. When they attempt to speak ill of our Black Communities, I will compassionately remind them of precious resources that exist within our Black Communities...but Black Community Compassion does not need a cosign. It stands on its own because it is true and intrinsically (from within) cultivated and manifested. Anyone that views it with a compassionate heart, regardless of ethnicity will celebrate its presence within the Black Community.

So, there it is...Black Self-Love. Not Hate but Love. Not with Discord but with Solidarity. Not with Unconcern but with Compassion. We need each other more than ever before. May we realize and recognize the Black Diamonds we are and even in their attempts to return us to coal...we remain powerful. The Diamonds are already Within Us. The Black Diamonds Are Us...even in the state of Black Coal. They cannot reverse what was brilliantly created and beautifully crafted!

WE ARE HERE! -Black Diamonds!

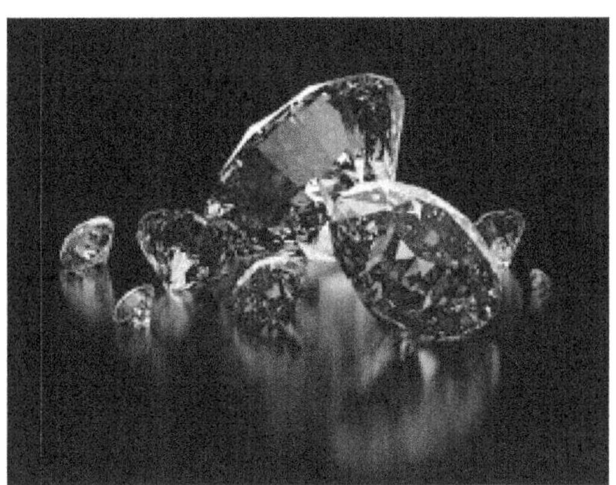

Good Vibes!

- **Take care of yourself like a precious stone. A one of a kind stone that deserves to sparkle in the light.**
- **Even in the state of coal, you are still worthy and valuable. You are going through a process of becoming a diamond.**

- **Love yourself, Love your community, and Allow Love to flow from your presence.**

**Good Thoughts:**

# About the Author

**Dr. Sconiers** is a Doctor of Social Work and a Licensed Clinical Social Worker. His passion work focuses on making Mental-Health & Wellness practical by merging Mental-Health and Wellness concepts with everyday emotions, life lessons, and moments of happiness we all desire.

**A word from the author:** Thank you for reading Good Vibes. I hope you found the greatness you possess within the passages. As always, please remember that Self-Care is not selfish but a necessary approach to living that will ensure that you are aware and recharging whenever you need it.

If you like the writings from Dr. Sconiers (Dr. S), check out his bestselling book. Good Mornings: Wake-Up Calls for Life is a daily positive read, packed with great messages to help you start your day!

Contact: Dr. Sconiers

Email: GoodVibeswithDr.S@gmail.com

Made in the USA
Middletown, DE
02 November 2023

41782106R00070